THE LIES WE TELL OURSELVES

A ONE-ACT PLAY

Franky Corcoran

THE LIES WE TELL OURSELVES

ISBN

PB: 978-1-7380475-2-9

ePUB: 978-1-7380475-3-6

First Printing, 2023

The Lies We Tell Ourselves was first staged on June 9, 2022 at the Beaverbrook Kin Centre by Corcoran Entertainment.

CAST

- VERN ANDERSON..Neil Wallace
- LIZA ANDERSON..Cynthia Gilks
- PEGGY BELL..Lisa Savage

- Lights/Sound..Ricky Barry
- Director...Franky Corcoran

THE LIES WE TELL OURSELVES

Setting:

(*A fancy hotel room. From left to right, there is a table and telephone. There is a king-sized bed and a dresser with an alarm clock, reading material and a lamp on top. A chair in the corner of the room. The bathroom is offstage to the right.*)

At Rise:

(*Newlyweds VERN and LIZA ANDERSON enter with luggage in hand. VERN wears a blue polo shirt and cargo shorts. LIZA wears a summer dress. VERN enters first, followed by LIZA.*)

VERN. Home sweet home.

LIZA. Those are three words I never thought I would hear you say coming back here.

VERN. No, I mean it. Say what you want about this city, but you really start to miss it. Especially when you've been gone for five years.

LIZA. Oh, of course. (*Sits on bed*) Wow. I might keep this bed all to myself tonight. We should have brought the cot for you.

VERN. (*Laughs with LIZA*) Certainly looks cozy. I hope you're not bummed about skipping Cuba?

LIZA. No. And even if I was, there's nothing I could do about it now. It was my fault regardless for not renewing my passport in time.

VERN. True, but then again, there's nothing worse than having to listen to those automated voices constantly reminding you that you're on hold. By the time you finally reach someone, you forget why you were calling them to begin with.

LIZA. And not to mention, this is much cheaper. Just a couple stops for gas is nothing compared to a plane flight. (*Enters bathroom*) Wow! This bathroom is *gorgeous!*

VERN. (*Looks into bathroom*) Are you seriously taking a bathroom selfie?

LIZA. Come on! I couldn't help it.

VERN. Maybe we just pack up our things and move right into this hotel room? So long, St. Andrews!

LIZA. It's pretty easy to tell how often I left St. Andrews. You probably think I'm overreacting.

VERN. Not in the slightest.

LIZA. (Runs *over to telephone.)* I've never used these fancy hotel phones before. *(Dials number and puts phone to her ear)* Hi Mom! Guess where I'm calling you from? ... Not the Empire State Building. I told you, my passport wasn't renewed in time. And besides, we were supposed to go to Cuba. Not New York. ... I'm in a hotel in Miramichi. ... It might not seem like that big of a deal, but you know how introverted I am when it comes to leaving the city.

VERN. Hi Mrs. LeBlanc!

LIZA. Vern says hi. ... Sure, one second. *(Hands telephone to VERN)*

VERN. *(Into telephone)* Hi, Mrs. LeBlanc, it's great to hear from you. … You sure I can call you Mom? I've only been your son-in-law for a full twenty-four hours now. Has enough time passed? … That works for me! … *(Loses his smile)* Oh?

LIZA. What?

VERN. Sure. Put him on. *(Covers phone)* Your dad wants to talk to me.

LIZA. Oh, Jesus. Just hang up. You don't have to.

VERN. No, no. It's okay. I am his son-in-law. Maybe he likes me now. *(Into phone)* Hello Mr. LeBlanc. … Mr. LeBlanc, *sir*. Right. My bad. … No, I didn't find my bank card. … We're married now. My bank card is her bank card and vice versa. We're in this together. … No, that won't be necessary. … Yes, you told me that at the altar. And when I asked for your blessings… Okay. *(Hands phone to LIZA and sits down, looking glum.)*

LIZA. *(Into phone)* Hi Dad. … Dad, I've told you countless times. As generous as it is, Vern and I are doing just fine without your financial support. … Dad, that's not nice. I don't even know why I called. Goodbye. *(Hangs up)*

VERN. The man hates me. What did I even do?

LIZA. He's your father-in-law. He's supposed to hate you.

VERN. But why? I asked for his blessings before I popped the question to you. He said it was okay… After he threatened to break my legs of course.

LIZA. Break your legs?

VERN. Said if I ever broke your heart, he'd break my legs.

LIZA. He's just overprotective. It's a father-daughter thing.

VERN. Protective? He's acting like I'm a juvenile delinquent. He says he "knows my type". What's my type?

LIZA. He's a retired cop who's bored. He's just looking for ways to keep busy and relive the glory days.

VERN. Did he do a background check on me? Does he know about my previous marriage?

LIZA. I only told him what you told me. Peggy cheated on you.

VERN. Right right.

LIZA. Dad's probably just not used to me being out and about. I never left St. Andrews before I met you. That's a good thing that came out of meeting you. I've finally broken out of my shell.

VERN. That's the *one* good thing? Only one?

LIZA. Well, that and the fact that we took your car and saved me some gas money.

VERN. Yeah. Even if I did spend every bit of cash that I had getting here.

LIZA. Why don't you try calling the bank again? Maybe they found your card?

VERN. Oh, what's the point? Their lines are so busy, it's like trying to renew your passport all over again.

LIZA. It's fine. Money isn't an issue. Let's just try and enjoy ourselves.

VERN. Enjoy ourselves? Knowing that some degenerate could be out blowing all of my hard earned money on God knows what?

LIZA. I'm sure it'll be fine.

VERN. My mother convinced me to get tap for my card. I told her no for this exact reason. Some thief gets ahold of my card, all they have to do is tap, tap, tap.

LIZA. Vern, Vern, Vern. Just calm down. *(Rubs his shoulders)* There you go. Don't go and get high blood pressure over this. What do you say we go get massages?

VERN. A massage? I don't know. What you're giving me is all I need.

LIZA. *(Laughs)* No! Downstairs. It's an all-inclusive hotel. Let's enjoy it while we're here.

VERN. That does sound pretty good. And Bay du Vin Days will be something to look forward to as well.

LIZA. *(Rolling her eyes)* Oh, right... That boat thing.

VERN. What are the odds, huh? What do you say we have a drink before we head down?

LIZA. Sure. What do we have?

VERN. *(Reaches into fridge and pulls out ice tray, a bottle of vodka)* Just vodka? Better than nothing I suppose. *(Pours vodka in two glasses and hands one to LIZA)* So... To the rest of our lives!

LIZA. *(Clinks glasses with VERN)* To the rest of our lives!

(Before they take a sip, there is rustling at the door. LIZA opens it to see a maid, PEGGY BELL standing there)

LIZA. Hi, can I help you?

PEGGY. Oh, I'm so sorry. I'm at the wrong room. I'm supposed-- *(Locks eyes with VERN)* Vern?

VERN. *(Spits vodka back into his glass)* Peggy? P-Patty?

PEGGY. Patty?

VERN. Patty, yes!

PEGGY. Patty?

VERN. Patty, yes!

LIZA. You two know each other?

VERN. Why yes. Patty and I go way back!

PEGGY. Who's Patty?

VERN. *(Laughing nervously)* You! Patty! This is my sister, Carrie's best friend, Patty... Patty Bellamy!

PEGGY. *(Confused)* Hi?

VERN. Patty, this is my wife, Liza. We just got married and we're here on our honeymoon.

LIZA. *(Shakes PEGGY's hand)* Hi, Patty. So nice to meet you.

PEGGY. Likewise. I-I apologize for interrupting. I was supposed to clean Room 405 following their checkout. I was off by one.

VERN. Checkout? Well, it would be a shame to checkout now. We just got here! *(Laughs nervously and takes a sip of his vodka)*

PEGGY. Well, my apologies, folks. Enjoy your stay. Good seeing you again, Vern. I hope *Carrie* is doing well.

VERN. She is. I'll let her know you send your regards. (*PEGGY exits*)

LIZA. Is it just me or was she acting paranoid?

VERN. Who, Peggy? No. She didn't seem paranoid to me.

LIZA. Who?

VERN. Who what?

LIZA. You just said Peggy. Isn't her name Patty?

VERN. Oh, yes, yes. My bad. No, she didn't seem paranoid to me. Not at all. *(Notices LIZA is skeptical)* I think you may be the paranoid one, darling.

LIZA. Maybe so. Anyways, how about those massages? First, let's do a proper toast this time.

VERN. You know what, honey? I'm pretty beat from the trip. I think I might stay back here and relax. You're welcome to join me.

LIZA. You're kidding me, right? We drove all the way here for over two hours just to *sleep?* Come on, Vern! This is our honeymoon. If this is all you wanted to do, we were better off just staying home!

VERN. I know. I'm pooped is all.

LIZA. *(Rubs VERN's shoulders)* But won't this be relaxing though?

VERN. But then that means I'd have to get up and walk all the way downstairs.

LIZA. You're so lazy you are!

VERN. It's not that. It's just that, we've been on the go since the reception hall. How about you go downstairs and I'll catch up in a little while?

LIZA. You want me to go down there all by myself and let some crackhead bum money off me for smokes and coffee? No thank you!

VERN. There won't be any of them here. If they can't afford two bucks for a coffee, then how do you expect them to spend one night at an all-inclusive hotel? *(Crosses to bed)* Unless you maybe want to wait a little bit, have some drinks with me?

LIZA. *(Angrily hands VERN her glass)* We're here to have fun, Vern. Just because you're tired, it doesn't mean I am too. Rest up and I'll see you later... Maybe. (*Exits*)

VERN. I love you, honey! *(She is already gone. He begins to hyperventilate.)* Oh, dear God. Oh my... Why? Why is this happening? *Is* this even happening? *(Slaps himself in the face and picks up the phone.)* Hello? ... Yes, I'd like a housekeeping service, please. It's an emergency ... Room 404. And may I request a specific housekeeper? ... There's only one working today? Oh, wonderful. Thank you so much. And hurry, please! *(Hangs up and finishes his drink and also LIZA's. He then grabs the bottle of vodka and drinks straight from the bottle. Moments later, there is a knock on the door.)* Okay, Vern... You got this. *(Opens the door to see PEGGY)*

PEGGY. Hello Mr. Anderson.

VERN. Peggy. Come in, would you?

PEGGY. *(Enters room)* Took you awhile, but I see you finally remembered my name. Now, can we make this quick? We're short staffed today and I have lots of work to do.

VERN. There was nothing to clean in here, Peggy. I just needed to talk to you.

PEGGY. Where's your wife?

VERN. She's downstairs getting a massage. I needed to talk to you before you expose me to her.

PEGGY. *(Offended)* Expose you? What makes you think I'd do that?

VERN. I don't know. My mind is just scrambling right now. Seeing you again, I-I feel like I'm dreaming. I just think that what Liza doesn't know won't hurt her. I'm not the same guy I was.

PEGGY. I'm surprised she's even giving you a chance after what you put me through. I take it she knows about that? *(VERN looks past her and is silent.)* She does know what happened, right?

VERN. Of course.

PEGGY. You're lying. I can tell. You never told her why we got divorced, didn't you?

VERN. Well, I may have embellished a tad.

PEGGY. How much is "a tad"?

VERN. She... She thinks you cheated on me.

PEGGY. She WHAT?!

(*There is a knock on the door*)

LIZA. *(Voice)* Vern? Can you open the door? You have my key.

VERN. *(Panicking)* Hide! Hide in the bathroom! Quick, quick! (*PEGGY runs in the bathroom. He opens the door.*) Hi, honey! Did you forget something?

LIZA. Yeah, I forgot my phone. I took that bathroom selfie and left it on the sink.

VERN. Oh, it's okay, honey. I'll grab it for you!

LIZA. No, it's okay. I can get it. I thought you were tired.

VERN. *(Tries to stop LIZA from getting to bathroom)* I am tired. I just... Those tacos from lunch finally caught up to me. *(Runs in bathroom, grabs her phone and hands it to her)* There you go, sweetheart!

LIZA. Thank you. Is everything okay?

VERN. Of course everything is okay. Why wouldn't it be?

LIZA. I don't know. You tell me.

VERN. Everything is just fine, honey. I promise. How about you get started on that massage and perhaps I'll join you after all?

LIZA. *(Suspicious)* Sure. *(Exits)*

VERN. Coast is clear!

PEGGY. *(Storms out of bathroom)* So, what did you tell her? You said that *I* cheated on *you?*

VERN. Like I said, I may have embellished the circumstances of our divorce--

PEGGY. Quit it with the real estate sales pitches! You're not fooling anybody now. You're painting this picture of me to your new wife that I'm some cheating bitch when in reality, *you're* the one who cheated!

VERN. Do you think I wanted to lie? Do you expect me to just live alone for the rest of my life? If I told her that when we first met, we wouldn't have gotten as far as we did!

PEGGY. You haven't changed a bit.

VERN. Yes, I've changed! Have I cheated on Liza? No. Ever since I met her, I have been on my best behavior.

PEGGY. But you're still a liar. How long have you two been together?

VERN. Our fourth anniversary of the day we met is tomorrow.

PEGGY. Four years? We got divorced five years ago. Didn't take you long to move on.

VERN. *(Thinks for a moment)* Can I ask you something? Why are you working here to begin with? It's a million in one chance that we'd reunite under these circumstances. What happened to your job at the nursing home?

PEGGY. The week the divorce was finalized, I was depressed. It was all that was on my mind, and I couldn't even do my job anymore. I was making mistakes. I even rear-ended a police car on the way to work one day. They let me go.

VERN. Are you serious?

PEGGY. Yes. I worked at a fast-food restaurant for six months. Worst experience of my life. Then I came here immediately after and I've been here ever since.

VERN. I hope you don't blame me for what happened.

PEGGY. I did blame you. For the next two years, all I did was curse your name.

VERN. I'm sorry, Peggy. I feel terrible.

PEGGY. Feeling terrible won't change what happened, but I'm glad you feel that way.

VERN. You really shouldn't blame me for losing your job. People go through bad things, but you can't let it define you. And you can't put the blame onto other people. You need to take responsibility for yourself.

PEGGY. *(Sarcastically)* What a valuable lesson! Thanks Barney.

VERN. I'm serious, Peggy!

PEGGY. Then tell me... Why did you sleep with Samantha?

VERN. W-What?

PEGGY. You heard me. Why did you sleep with Samantha?

VERN. *(Nervous)* Oh, Peggy... I-I think that's nonsense--

PEGGY. *(Impatient)* Why is it nonsense? I asked you a very simple question. Why. Did. You. Sleep. With. Samantha?

VERN. *Because I was stressed out, okay?!* You know what I was dealing with at the time. All the bullshit I had going on at the office, those deals on the properties not going through. I had lots on my mind and you were never around!

PEGGY. Is that really what you think?

VERN. That's what I know.

PEGGY. Do you remember when my mom died?

VERN. What does that have to do with this?

PEGGY. I didn't even get to say goodbye to her. The last time I saw her, we had a fight about something childish. Little did I know that I would never see her again. Then six months later, my husband cheats on me with my best friend, we get divorced, I lost my job, but does that make it okay to hurt people?

VERN. Maybe it doesn't. Did that really happen? You fought with your mom?

PEGGY. *(Infuriated) Yes that happened!* Not like you ever cared enough to ask.

VERN. Well, I'm sorry! If only you were around to comfort *me* when I needed it.

PEGGY. What the hell are you even talking about? *When* were you even struggling? You were completely fine and then one day, out of blue, I drove by Samantha's house and whose car is parked in her driveway, but yours? If I never drove by, would you have confessed? *(VERN is silent)* You see? You haven't changed at all. You're a lying scumbag. You're selfish and you're a coward. You go on and on about how I should take responsibility for my own mistakes and yet you can't even do the same. You can excuse cheating on your wife by making it about "coping with work stress" like that makes it any better. And then you destroy my self image just to better yours! You make me sick, *Vernon!*

VERN. *(Feels defeated)* I'm sorry, Peggy. I really am. *(Sits on bed)* I left Miramichi to start over. I found a fresh start in St. Andrews. I was hoping that coming back here, it would be a way of leaving the past in the past and starting over fresh.

PEGGY. You can't *not* face up to your mistakes and expect everything to work out. Liza may have helped change, but you can't always rely on other people to do that for you. *You* need to make those decisions for yourself.

VERN. We should tell Liza the truth. Me and you both.

PEGGY. I'm not doing your dirty work for you.

VERN. Why not?

PEGGY. Out with old, in with the new. If you have me tell the truth for you, it shows that you're still a coward.

VERN. *(Beat.)* Do you mind if I ask how things are?

PEGGY. Meaning?

VERN. You know what I mean. Come on. How have you been?

PEGGY. Good, good. I'm a step-mom now actually.

VERN. Really? That's great!

PEGGY. Thank you. My boyfriend Charles has two kids. Seven-year old girl and a four-year old son. They're a barrel of laughs.

VERN. Remember that time we babysat my cousin Abby when her parents went to Vancouver? You and I never changed a diaper before and of course, she had to crap *everywhere!*

PEGGY. *(Laughing)* Yes, I remember.

VERN. I will never forget when her parents came home. Talk about terrible timing!

PEGGY. *(Her laugh abruptly stops)* Vern, what are you doing?

VERN. Just reminiscing. Is that okay?

PEGGY. Go ahead. Because if you're serious about changing, your life will be completely different by this time tomorrow.

VERN. Before that happens, I have to ask you something. After everything I did to you, why are you helping me now?

PEGGY. Because I can't help but wonder if there's even a shred of hope left for you to change.

VERN. You don't have to help me, Peggy.

PEGGY. I know. But I spent years with you. Despite

everything that happened, you'd be surprised to know that I still do care about you. I know the man I first fell in love with is still inside of you somewhere, but you have to *want* to let him out.

VERN. Thank you.

PEGGY. Just don't get the wrong idea. We're not friends. I'm mainly doing this, so your poor wife doesn't have to go through the same thing I did. I have to get back to work. *(Walks to door. She stops and turns around.)* It was nice seeing you again, Vern.

VERN. You too, Peg.

(PEGGY opens the door to see LIZA there, about to knock. VERN and PEGGY are both speechless.)

LIZA. *(Confused and enters)* Hello Patty. What brings you back up here?

PEGGY. *(Stammering)* I was... I-I... Well, it turns out that... That this *was* the right room to clean!

VERN. Yes! That's right! Remember when she was up here looking to clean Room 405, but it turns out that it *was* Room 404.

PEGGY. *(Overlapping with VERN)* That's right! One of those days, huh? I think we all have those.

LIZA. *(Raises her voice)* Alright, everyone! Stop talking for a minute!

VERN. *(A brief silence)* That was a quick massage.

LIZA. I didn't get one. Between the time I left to get my phone and go back down, some fat pig and her friends came strutting in with her friends and took my spot. I wasn't in the mood to wait.

PEGGY. I'm sorry to hear that. Ashley down there gives excellent massages--

LIZA. *(Puts her finger to PEGGY's lips and shushes her)* What is going on in here?

VERN. Nothing.

LIZA. Do you really think I'm that stupid?

VERN. I didn't say you were stupid. I just said there's nothing going on here. Can't Peggy just do her job so she can pay her bills?

LIZA. Peggy?

VERN. Did I say Peggy? I-I meant Patty! Can't Patty do her job so she can pay her bills and make a living?

PEGGY. It's okay, guys. I'll just go. The room looks clean to me now. Goodbye! *(Runs for the door)*

LIZA. Hold it! *(PEGGY stops)* None of this crap is adding up and nobody is going anywhere until I get to the bottom of it.

VERN. What crap isn't adding up?

LIZA. Well, how about the one you took in the bathroom before I came in? You never seemed to worry about hiding *that* from me before, did you?

VERN. Are we seriously arguing about my bowel movements?

PEGGY. *Oh my God! I cannot take this anymore!* Liza, there's something you need to know.

VERN. Peggy, don't!

LIZA. Peggy?

VERN. Sorry! Patty!

PEGGY. *Stop it!* My name is not Patty! My name is Peggy Bell. The ex-wife!

(LIZA's heart is shattered into a million pieces. She collapses onto the bed.)

VERN. Liza, dear! Liza, please! I swear it's not what you think it is!

LIZA. *(Choked up)* How can I believe a single word you say?

VERN. Honey, listen to me. There is nothing going on between Peggy and me. This is all one big misunderstanding.

LIZA. One big misunderstanding? Your behavior right now is enough evidence to prove that you're not being sincere.

PEGGY. He's telling you the truth, Liza. Just not the truth you're thinking of.

LIZA. What the hell is that supposed to mean?

VERN. Liza, dear... Peggy didn't cheat on me. *I* cheated on Peggy.

LIZA. *(Dumbfounded)* What? So now, you're cheating on me with *her?! (Gets up and tries to charge at PEGGY, but VERN stops her.)*

VERN. No! Would you just listen to me, please? *(Sits LIZA back on the bed and sits next to her)* I had a tendency to cope with my own problems and insecurities by doing terrible things and then blame it on me being stressed out. That's what I did to Peggy. Sure, I may have been stressed over my work, but she always seemed so busy and I felt like I could never open up to her about any of this stuff. Her best friend, Samantha was vulnerable at the time because she had just divorced her husband. To make a long story short, I would go over to Samantha's everyday after work and...

Well, you know. *(LIZA buries her face in her hands)* Of course, Peggy had to find out about it. She didn't even have to elicit a confession out of me. She just drove by Samantha's after work one day and saw my car parked outside. She threw me out, I lost all of my friends' respect for it because of what happened.

LIZA. Good grief. And yet you still wanted to come here for our honeymoon.

VERN. I didn't want to live in fear for the rest of my life. I'd hyperventilate just hearing the word, "Miramichi". This was all a part of me turning over a new leaf. Perhaps this was bound to happen sooner or later.

PEGGY. There's the Vern I know.

LIZA. Hey, keep your eyes off him, honey.

PEGGY. You know what I mean. *This* Vern is one of the most honest people you will ever know. I knew he was still in there somewhere.

VERN. Peggy, I'm sorry. It must have taken you awhile to start a new relationship after what I did.

PEGGY. Well, not really. What took me awhile was feeling comfortable again. Anytime Charles would say he was going for a drive, or going out with friends, I'd stay home and have an anxiety attack. I even had to seek counselling.

VERN. I didn't know that.

PEGGY. I'm sure you felt bad enough about what you did. I didn't want to make you feel worse.

LIZA. *(Takes VERN's hand)* I forgive you, Vern. You lied for the right reasons. Now we can start over.

VERN. Well, I'm sorry, Liza... But I don't think this marriage is going to work out.

LIZA. *(Heartbroken)* Wait, what? Why?!

VERN. Because the trust is gone. I can't bear the thought of living our lives while you're worried about what I'm hiding from you. I can't put someone through that again.

LIZA. But it's fine, Vern. Really! We can get through this.

VERN. You say that now, but it's much easier said than done. We would just be delaying the inevitable.

LIZA. Vern, are you serious about this? I mean, we haven't been married a full twenty-four hours and we're out of town!

VERN. I understand the timing isn't ideal, but you'll thank me later.

LIZA. *(In tears)* Where do we go from here?

VERN. We'll spend the night here and try to enjoy the night.

LIZA. How can we? *We're getting a divorce!*

VERN. *(Walks to the door)*

PEGGY. *(Stops VERN)* Vern, what are you doing?

VERN. I'm going for a walk.

PEGGY. You're really just walking out on your wife?

VERN. You wanted me to be honest so Liza didn't go through what you did. If I'm a truly changed man, then my slate needs to be wiped clean.

PEGGY. She forgave you. She loves you unconditionally. You're going to walk out on her still?

VERN. Trust me. I'm doing her a favor. *(Exits.)*

(PEGGY looks at LIZA, who is crying on the bed. She goes to sit beside her but decides against it. She instead pulls up a chair from the corner of the room.)

PEGGY. You probably don't want to hear this, especially from me. But this is probably for the best.

LIZA. I'm starting to wonder what I ever saw in him to begin with. I don't care about him lying to me. Everyone has secrets. This was supposed to be a fresh start.

PEGGY. We were married four and a half years. Back then, I will admit that I was blind to a lot of his antics. Love does something to you. When we got married, he was so charming. You couldn't not love him. But there were all these pieces of the puzzle that I didn't put together until the divorce. Like, we only hung out with my friends once. *Only once!* We were hanging out with his friends every damn weekend. It didn't bother me then because I was so in love with him. But now, I understand why my friends never wanted much to do with me after our wedding. It was all him.

LIZA. *(To herself)* "I know his type..." Oh, Dad.

PEGGY. I'm sorry?

LIZA. My dad. He was always skeptical of who he was. Perhaps if I had just listened to him right from the start, maybe none of this would have happened.

PEGGY. Don't blame yourself.

LIZA. We're a lot alike in many ways. I just wish I didn't have to learn all this the hard way.

PEGGY. I didn't mean to put you in this position. I am so sorry. Just seeing him again after I finally improved things in my life, I started to spiral. The second I laid eyes on him, it felt like all the mental progress I made just disappeared. I was just trying to save you the heartbreak.

LIZA. You have nothing to be sorry about.

PEGGY. *(Sits next to LIZA)* Listen, we don't have to be friends, but I just don't want there to be any hard feelings between us. If anything, I would say you're lucky that you aren't wasting years away of your life like I did.

LIZA. Thank you. *(Smiles at PEGGY, who smiles back.)*

(VERN enters.)

LIZA & PEGGY. What is it, Vern?

VERN. Liza, I'm so sorry. I made such a mistake. I should have told you sooner, but...

LIZA. What?

VERN. *(Reaches into pocket and pulls out card)* I had my debit card the entire time.

(Blackout.)

End of Play.

NOTES:

www.ingramcontent.com/pod-product-compliance
Lightning Source LLC
Chambersburg PA
CBHW071400200726
48294CB00004B/1231
* 9 7 8 1 7 3 8 0 4 7 5 2 9 *